Slurping Soup

Written and Illustrated
by
Kelly Kennedy

ENTER

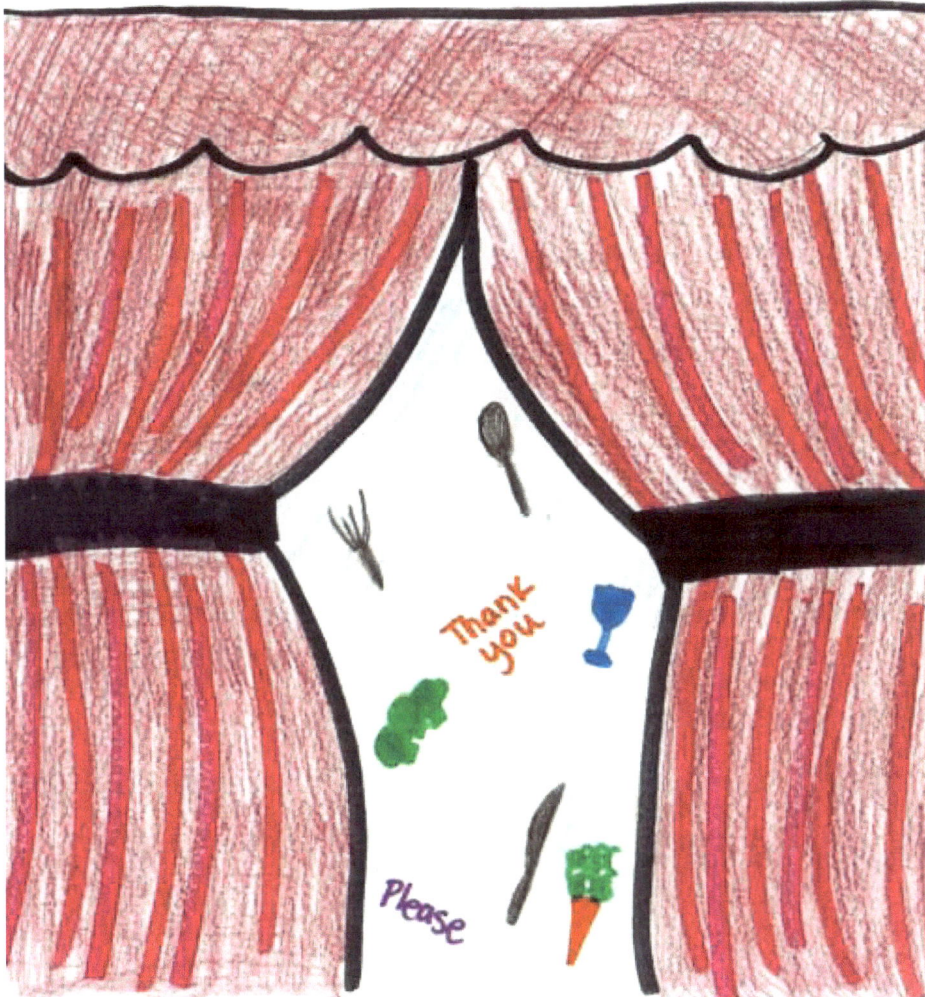

Table manners are important to learn,
and so now it is your turn.

You will use them everyday of your life.
Every time you pick up a
spoon, fork, or knife.

How to set the table,
is where we will start.

Making it perfect is a special art.

Fork to the LEFT,
knife and spoon to the RIGHT.

napkin

Left

Left

You are almost ready,
to take your first bite.

Do not eat with your fingers food like pork.
That is why they invented the spoon, knife, and fork

When chewing your food,
keep your mouth shut.

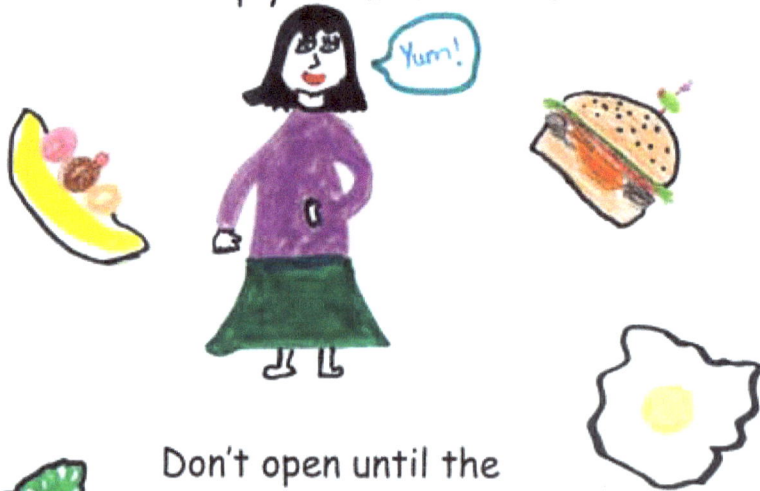

Yum!

Don't open until the
food hits your gut.

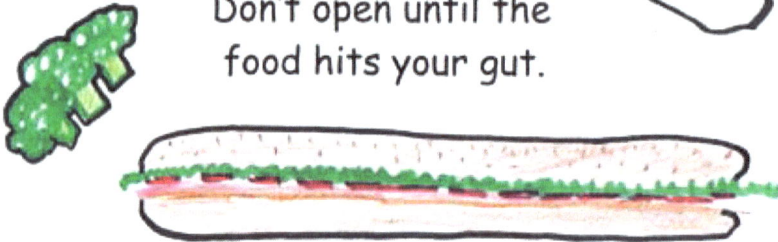

Grapes

bananas

broccoli

Eat veggies and fruit
to stay healthy and strong.
When you go to school,
bring them along.

carrots

oranges

strawberries

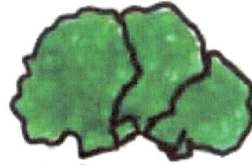

Spinach

Pineapple

Apples

ATTENTION DOG OWNERS:

Don't feed the dog at your feet.
Human food is not a treat.

Bark Bark

They make food for the dog.
He shouldn't act like a hog.

Oink
Oink

When eating hot soup, do not slurp.
Also do not ever burp.
Others at the table will think you are rude.
Not to mention these habits are very crude.

Always place the napkin on your lap.
For then it will act as a food trap.

If the food you want is too far away,
politely ask someone to pass it your way.

Please

Thank
you

Anybody is able,
to reach across the table.
But, it is very rude,
to reach for the food.

Pass Food
to your
Left

If you accidentally drip food on your chin,

politely wipe it off with your napkin.

Keep your elbows off the table
every time you eat.

Also don't pick your
teeth or feet.

After the meal,
parents might ask you to clean.

SOAP

Sink

Always say yes,
and never be mean.

Remember your manners as you grow.

Whether at the dinner table,
or out on the go.

Once these manners are learned and done,

eating dinner will be much more fun!!

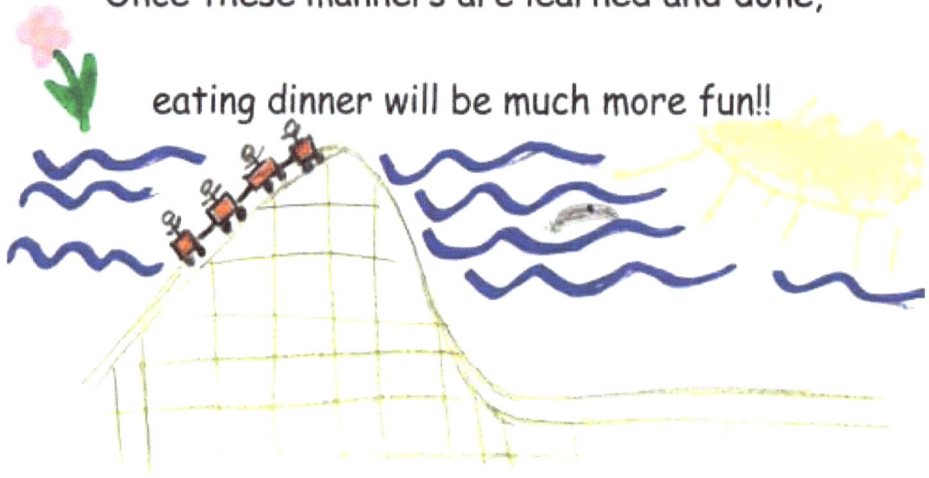

THE

END

Extra...

Be nice to everybody you meet through the day.

Everyone is special, in his or her own perfect way.

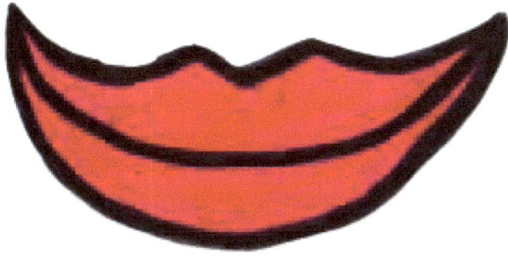

REMEMBER:

A smile can go a very long way!

www.ingramcontent.com/pod-product-compliance
Lightning Source LLC
Chambersburg PA
CBHW060855270326
41934CB00002B/150